The Man with the Dancing Monkey

The Man with the Dancing Monkey

Barbara Curry Mulcahy

Wolsak and Wynn . Toronto

Copyright © Barbara Curry Mulcahy, 1997

All rights reserved. No part of this book may be reproduced or transmitted in any form, by any means, electronic or mechanical, without permission in writing from the publisher, except by a reviewer who may quote brief passages in a review.

Typeset in Palatino, printed in Canada by
The Coach House Printing Company, Toronto

Front cover art: "The Man with the Dancing Monkey" in oil pastel and charcoal, with kind permission of the artist, © Brian Donald Hohner
Cover design: Stan Bevington
Author's Photograph: Mike Mulcahy

Some of these poems were first published in these or earlier forms in *200% Cracked Wheat*, *blue buffalo*, *Introductions from an Island 1975*, *The Antigonish Review*, *dandelion*, *Event*, *Grain*, *Quarry*, *Other Voices*, *The NeWest Review*, *Skylines*, and *Poetry Canada Review*.

The author wishes to acknowledge her gratitude to The Alberta Foundation for the Literary Arts and to Alberta Culture and Multiculturalism for financial assistance. She also wishes to thank John Glenday, Tom Wayman, Andrew Wreggitt, Di Brandt and the writers in residence at the University of Alberta for their advice and encouragement.

The publishers gratefully acknowledge support from The Canada Council and The Ontario Arts Council which made publication of this book possible.

Wolsak and Wynn Publishers Ltd.
Don Mills Post Office Box 316
Don Mills, Ontario, Canada, M3C 2S7

Canadian Cataloguing in Publication Data

Mulcahy, Barbara, 1954-
  The man with the dancing monkey
Poems.
ISBN 0-919897-54-1
I. Title.
PS8576.U38M36 1997   C811'.54   C97-930645-0
PR9199.3.M75M36 1997

For Mike

CONTENTS

listen

THREE BEGINNINGS

1
Silk / 13
On a dark mountain / 14
Ice / 15
Three beginnings / 16
The man with the dancing monkey / 17
Shore / 18
The chair / 19

2
The garden of the man whose wife has left him / 21
Narrows / 22
Picking roots / 23
The hunting knife / 24
Sanctuary / 25
Muskeg / 26
Season of the winter solstice / 28
Colostrum / 29
paddler desires / 30

3
My muse is a tramp / 31
Like my father / 32
Grandmother / 34
Learning / 35
The hunter's tale / 36
Night round of the multipara / 37
Passage / 38
Belief / 39
I see my son wait to recite a poem / 41
differences / 42
My muse is tired of literature / 43

RAVEN MEDITATIONS

1
The thing about the raven ... / 47
The raven is loud and ... / 48
For some birds it's a struggle ... / 49
The owl has padded wings ... / 50
So what ... / 51
A squad of ravens ... / 52
The falcon ... / 53
I could put it ... / 54
After the end of the world ... / 55
Ravens are the remnants ... / 56
"You have the cold-hearted ... / 57
The raven walks ... / 58
Dominus vobiscum ... / 59

2
Bury me on a platform ... / 61
A temporary structure will do ... / 62
It will be hard ... / 63
bury me ... / 64

3
You! Raven! ... / 65
if I were a raven ... / 66
Winter ... / 67
Why do I look elsewhere ... / 68
Snow, and more snow ... / 69

4
Why did ... / 71
Love is the size ... / 72
Love is the shape ... / 73
love is the colour ... / 74
with what big wings ... / 75

                    listen

                    this is
        love
                    this necessary
        rip

        the world emerges
                    what   was
        is dust

        let it lift
                          and settle
        lift
                          and settle

THREE BEGINNINGS

SILK

We are clumsy: the cocoons crumple.
We cannot find the beginning.
"The worms have fed on mulberry leaves. Men bring the cocoons in truckloads from the country," they tell us, as if this were the answer.

In front of them, vats of hot water. Cocoons float; the water steams.
And the women: their reddened faces, arms, and their hands — puffy and wrinkled as sleeves.
And fast — as soon as they grab a cocoon out of the water the thread is loose, attached to the end of the last thread. Such a long filament, unreeling.

All that is left is the wet shell and inside a dead worm.

In the unlit workroom, the women laugh and talk. Their faces are wet and as they reach we see wet hair in their armpits.

The water is so hot we can't put our hands in long enough to grab even one cocoon. We look at the women with amazement. They laugh. "You are young," they say.

The pile of cocoon shells is to one side. We select a few dry ones.
They are impossible to open. They don't break.
But you can shake the sarcophagus and hear its dead worm rattle.

The pile gleams, the most silvery silken light. The great door is open and the cocoons transform the light reflected into the room. They are in the shade but they gleam. Moonshine. Each cocoon wrapped in the finest thread and laden with a fat living worm. The piles dumped here. And now and then a fat worm moves and its cocoon shifts and the pile of ovals shifts, slides down, and the base of the pile widens, or else one or two cocoons spill out across the dusty floor, into bright sunlight.

ON A DARK MOUNTAIN

On a dark mountain, a stone
falls. The cliffs accept
the sound of its falling; the earth
accepts the sound of the stone.

On a dark mountain, pine trees
support themselves on the pressure.
A stream discovers itself for the last
time against these rocks.

Like a rake, the water turns
a stone, over and over.

ICE

1.
"Ice! Ice!"
Burlap on the big blocks of ice in the donkey cart
and a wet trail on the dusty road.

A housewife calls from her window. It's
sensuous — the way she screams. A parrot
would call like this, a crow.

The man ties the reins to a tree. Uncovers the ice.
With metal prongs, he stabs —
grabs a block.

Each hand clasps
a set of prongs
that clasp a block of ice.

2.
The cart drips. The donkey waits.
He has old black blinders
on his eyes.

The tongs clatter into the cart. The man
unties the reins, slaps them on the donkey's back.
"Ice! Ice!"

The donkey does not move. Ladies
down the street laugh.
The ice man takes his stick.

"Thwack! Thwack!"
on the donkey's back.
The donkey brays loudly.

THREE BEGINNINGS

Wait like a silverfish dry and boneless.
Wait with legs and the castanet
back of a beetle. Wait in the woollen cowl
of the sky.

The wind like a mountain; like the arched spine
of a mountain; like a mountain; like the sparrow-bone caves
of a mountain; like a mountain; like a wounded
tiger. The wind.

The petiole's base is broken
like the hoof of a horse at the top
of a hill. The rain on the window is broken
like the hoof of a horse at the top
of a hill: the horse, the horse, the horse
on the hill.

THE MAN WITH THE DANCING MONKEY

plays an accordion and the monkey
dances on a leash.

The monkey wears a little red jacket
with pockets and gold braid. He has pants on
and a special hole for his long tail —
maybe for other things too.

His tail is long as a peacock's feather.
It curls at the end where it rests on the path.
From it, the monkey dances like a marionette — except —
out of step with the music.

The music, the rinky-tink happiness!

But the monkey is tired, he leans on his tail.
He hops and claps his little black leather palms
while the man plays. When the music stops,
the monkey climbs the man and takes his cap.
He hops down and holds the cap up.
His eyes are big and he looks tired.
The man looks tired too.

He and the monkey wear matching clothes — except —
for the man — no hole, no tail to lean on.

Dawn. The sky ... rippled, a bedcover ...
A sand spit covered with bird tracks, the birds
out feeding from the ocean.

Noon. The water sounding ... the sway of a pregnant woman's
hips. Thrust
and slide, thrust
and slide, and a mussel closes its lips
on the blue elastic water.

Afternoon. Back in
on itself the ocean collapses and the sun fades
back into the sky and the sky quivers
like a bowstring tightening
back into itself.

Dusk. Covered with
bird-call, the ocean, the land and ...
in the night, waves and flight.

THE CHAIR

The chair in the room
In which you lie.
The chair,
The arm of the chair
In the room in which you lie
Is fluted
By the pacing of my fingers.

The chair,
The chair in the room
In which you lie.
The chair,
The creak of the chair
In the room in which you lie
As I move to grasp
Your hand.
Your hand: skin
Fluted between leaping veins.

THE GARDEN OF THE MAN WHOSE WIFE HAS LEFT HIM

Her unthinned flower beds are distended with weeds,
but still the perennials compete, flashing,
summer after summer, like lighthouse
beacons. And the daisies spread into the lawn
until he can mow it only in the evening
when his eyesight is riddled with the low sunshine
and his mind is flaccid with beer.

Among the vegetables is a row of lettuce thick
with her absence, each surplus leaf a green memory
until frost rots the heads and he tills them under.

NARROWS

        I would be lake
      but I have tumbled
          out of that
and now there's no point in what
       isn't   It's rocks
and constrictions and standing   waves
    and eddies we can turn
    into   if we are accurate
      at the right time

        And why is it
when all the words have been
   used have been ground
      down why is it
when there is nothing left
     that I look back
    and want you so
       clearly
   I would   be lake

PICKING ROOTS

Now we pick roots from the field
to burn in the long fire,
long flexible roots that we have to wind up
out of the earth
and short clubs matted
with the clay soil.
We move in separate circles,
gather wood for a fire
whose flames we will watch,
flames leashed to the soil
but striking out at the air.

THE HUNTING KNIFE

I wash the hunting knife,

scour the rust,
polish off the strange dark
colours.

It was a gift from your father
who still thinks
that you will go out one day
for your own meat.

Beautiful knife,
heavy and sharp. The blade
curves in the air
the way   you   curve
in me.

After arguments like this,
when you have sheathed yourself in silence
and I have withdrawn
against you, there is still a part of me
that wants to be hunted —
wants to be opened, to steam
like guts into a fall day,
hanging from this cavity,
exposed for love.

SANCTUARY

I want to lie down by the side
of the farrowing sow
enclosed in the barn
on a winter night. Dung
freezes to the floor
by the outside wall;
broken stalks
in the nest of fresh straw
remind me to stillness.
The heat lamp glows
in the creep in the corner
of the stall. The farrowing sow
eases her litter to warmth
and sound. The small barn
embedded in the dark:
the rhythm of silence
and then that whole
rebounding chant
as each sow
grunts her litter
to suck.

MUSKEG

1.
Muskeg burns all winter, beneath the snow, beneath our feet —
and the air so cold I only look out at it. What I exhale sweats under
my scarves. And the ground burns beneath us, your eyelashes singed
white, your mustache thick with frost.

Does it matter that we cannot see the smoke, that the ground
smoulders below? I would hold your hand, your mitt, if I were not so
cold, so tired of cold.

2.
The time I hit you. The way you stood there, just stood, and I
felt I loved you so much I could never hurt you   enough.

3.
don't confuse me with love
I'm sick of all this blow-by
fumes from an old engine
the strength you have to have —
breath you feel and the heart hides
like it always does
safe

4.
This distance between us, this distance. No reasons, thought —
another separation, and you look out — meltwater, a skiff of snow, on
and on it goes.

5.
and I cannot give, in casting I only cast inward, I am unable to cast
away, I am unfaithful

take away this only thing that is, tear me out of what I cannot give

your arms, the hair on your arms, the hair on the nape of your neck,
the hair that I hold in my hands

6.
Which lie do you want?
That there is no love,
that you won't feel it
or that it doesn't hurt?

Nothing survives and you have to
give yourself,
moment by moment,
piece by piece, give yourself.

7.
begin. again. branches. ice fog, more beautiful than leaves. a small
warm room and windows and snow and a hill and your body.

all the ways I wanted you, the ways I wanted to want you, that I
wanted to want. abstractions. declensions —
the endless procession.

your body, my body, this small warm room.
I inhabit you. and the snow on the hillside also.

8.
The snow collapses. Such noise beneath. Birch, poplar, pine, alder,
spruce, willow, tamarack. Fresh snow, fresh tracks.

You want to show me what I've heard so many times. This. The
moon, a full moon, rises behind the spruce.

Air slices into the lungs, snow cracks apart at each step, sound slips unsheathed from foot to masked ear.
What is — is lineal.

The straw-stubbled snow, the cold-forged poplars, comes the noise of the train — of its wheels, of its whistle, of its engine.
Unfettered, this sound.

Between steps, wheels and whistle: the eye. Sunlight halos a leaf dangling from its stalk. Sound and ear; leaf and eye.
Long shadows blue the snow.

She looks for her kid. She saw him carried away. She calls out as I milk her little teats — the colostrum thick as it always is, creamy.

I move my shoulder forward against her ribs to steady her against the stall. The stream jets out in the light, knotted with pressure.

Then she moves again and I shove farther into her. My face anchors into her smooth fur. It smells like summer — the alfalfa that she's pulled from her manger for a nest.

rocks, bones to slide over with the mushy bottom of his polyethylene canoe. hips and ribs, wrists, finger bones, femurs and tension. motion and the current   that electrical leap to synapse.

confluence. wide water without rock. from side to side, read for current.

islands in the bends of the river. a prow of driftwood left from break-up. long gravel beaches and, when the island's high enough, the old forest — what didn't burn. old birch, old spruce, and those silicate horsetails he uses to scrub the fry-pan.

night. river rises. they've let water out of the dam. dawn. his canoe at the edge, tied to wild alfalfa. rocks submerged. he sees the edges have come forward; he pulls the canoe to shore, loads it, enters.

silt ping. the dark river, the clay-dark river.

MY MUSE IS A TRAMP

My muse has a beehive hairdo; she uses my pencils to scratch her scalp. "This writing," she says, "it's not healthy." She gives me a list of what I need. Red lipstick. Eyeliner. Evening in Paris eau de cologne. "It comes in a blue bottle," she tells me.

I shut the window and the door when my muse visits because she has a loud voice that proclaims, for example, "PEOPLE LIKE SEX" and "DON'T BE DUTIFUL." But when I write down these instructions she acts exasperated.

My muse is a tramp; when a man walks in the room she forgets all about me. Sometimes she walks out with him. "Scritch, scritch" her stockings say and her stiletto heels give her strong stride just the faintest hint of instability.

My muse comes back to me laughing and at ease. She sits on my desk and lassoes me with her smoke rings. Her shiny stockings go "scritch, scritch" when she shifts her hips. I know they're stockings, not pantyhose, because she pulls up her skirt and adjusts her garters. She sees me watch her. She looks at my papers and shakes her head. "Your writing," she says, "suffers from a lack of lingerie."

LIKE MY FATHER

What I would give
to swear like my father —
the cognac in his snifter rolls
like mercury. The colours cupped in his hand
glow and disappear as he ranges in and out of the light
shed through the doorway. "Shit,"
he says, "it's all tendentious
horseshit. Betty —
I need another drink."

My mother, in the living room,
at cards, says, "Then
get one." And to me, "Full house."
She passes the latest box of chocolates
that my father's brought.
My mother is generous
with her chocolates, and why not? —
she doesn't like them.

My father says, "I came here searching the
"wine-dark" sea —
and what do I find on this shore?
Another brown-nose bureaucracy."

My mother shuffles the cards.

"Betty," he calls,
"come here." My mother
hands out the deck. "Betty,"
he calls, "look
at this
sky." My mother
doesn't say anything but she lays down her hand and goes
to the screen door. I follow her.
We walk out on the patio.

There is a smell from the garden
and the fields around us and the sky
is filled with stars that look like pinpricks in a dark
lampshade. "How about that?" my father says.
"Lift up thine eyes, etcetera."

GRANDMOTHER

I kick one leg over the wool blanket's cold rough twill, hear her.

Her hands. The beads. Her chant:
> Hail Mary
> Full of grace
> The Lord is with Thee.

She turns; the bed creaks. Her voice rises. The words:
> Blessed art Thou
> Amongst women
> Blessed is the fruit
> Of Thy womb: Jesus.

Her voice breaks. Mucus rasps from her throat into her white handkerchief. I peek: she bunches the cloth, places it inside the pillowcase.
> Holy Mary
> Mother of God
> Pray for us
> Sinners
>
> Now
> And at the hour
> Of our death.

Through knotholes, through open slots, between sliding boards, I see it: her nightgown — white and shiny. One strap fallen from a shoulder — smooth against thick and folded flesh.

Lace around her breasts. And between them, wrinkles seeping down.

LEARNING

"Jesus—," I say, stifling
the rest for his sake
but my son
catches me checking him
and thinks I am bound up
again. "—Christ," he prompts,
and his manner — relaxed,
assisting — as if he were passing me salt,
irritates me. "I can swear by myself,"
I snap. And it's the
astonishment, the
pleasure as he says, "I didn't know
it was swearing."

You know how it is when you skin a bear, what comes out is a man. You hang him up — paws and claws pinned high and all the rest of him, muscular — so human, so stretched out, it makes you sick.

So I don't hunt. If I want meat, I eat something dumb — something with wings.

I wake in the dark, feel brittle, achy as an old lady. I roll over, sit up. Then, using my arms to push off, I rise. First, to the bathroom, passing the light left on in the hall to mark the hazard of trucks and building blocks.

Then, the children. It's hardly necessary but I adjust their covers, tuck an errant foot into a crib, and, in doing this, am enveloped in the way they sleep — so purely that when I watch I hyperventilate — become dizzy and have to kneel for a moment, have to touch my head to the floor. And it's like being punched, the way the baby shoves into my stomach. I rise, shut the door, go back into the dark living-room where the light from the hall turns the windows into mirrors, where I see myself whole, swollen and restless.

I turn on the overhead light, pick up toys, put away shoes, hang up the jackets and scarves. I squat for each abandoned object, exhale as I rise. My hips loose, rattle almost in their pods. I move slowly, grasp windowsills to pull myself up, rest against the walls. Youth, beauty, flexibility discarded like petals. Belly swollen hard like a rose hip, and all around — frost ripens, softens, readies us.

PASSAGE

Conception

Was it the bird at the open
window, the sun in the shunting
clouds? The top of a cedar paused
as the wind was breathed back
in.

You, my trajectile in this void, spin
with the force of blood, of sunlight centred.

Below my breasts,
under my belly, silence pushes.

The Second Trimester

In the night you make angel wings
in this cradle. My heart is a rocking chair
and I hold you with the corseting muscles of my stomach, touching
bottom, touching down
in this firm flesh where I too, have been planted.

Miscarriage

The silhouette of a seagull
flies out over the ocean, into
the sun. Two wings, shells,
open, open, then scud
shut.

Somewhere in the fullness of night, in the fullness
of the moon, the tide breaks
on this beach, on a cedar
peeling in the surf.

BELIEF

I, too,
believe
in the Easter Bunny.
April full of mud and wind.
The roof resounds with each thrust.

We decorate eggs,
keep them fresh
in baskets in the fridge.

The night before Easter
the Bunny comes,
chains on his tires
or maybe using his 4 x 4.

He wears gum rubbers,
leaves footprints side by side,
puts his boots by the door, then,
takes all the eggs
and hides them.

The psychiatrists say
it's a perversion
of the drive that rabbits
are famous for.

But the Easter Bunny
is like a grandmother, he doesn't
care. He is talking to himself,
saying, "In the boots?
No, that was last year.
Under the pillow? Yes,
every year. In the teddy bear's arms?
Yes."

Softly, he hops around the house,
the linoleum cool on his padded paws.
He sheds long white winter fur
here and there on the furniture.

When the eggs are gone,
he fills the baskets
with all the things I do not
allow: chocolate replicas of himself,
expensive
little
foil-wrapped hollow eggs,
jelly beans that gum in your teeth.
He brings chalk
and caps for the toy guns.
He is like a grandmother;
he has no sense.

I SEE MY SON WAIT TO RECITE A POEM

He stands there at the front of the class,
seven years old ...

and I look into water, the image
wavers, time — a heat streamer
rises off a lake, dislocates my features
into his.

That familiar expression, that same damned earnest
intensity; in doubt
and relentless,
he wants and cannot speak.

He waits just below the surface of language.

DIFFERENCES

because you are hairy
and I am smooth
and there is something
intriguing
about that
because you dangle
and I do not
because you growl and I twitter
because you smell and I
well   maybe I smell   too
but anyway
not so much
because you are bigger
and stronger
and have to hold yourself back
because you tell me you would become a Jehovah Witness
if it would end your pain
because you would believe in miracles
because already   you believe
in things
that work
because you are big and hairy and growl and smell and would believe
                               in false gods and miracles and machines
because you dangle
for all these reasons
and more
you are very interesting
to me

My muse is tired of being invoked by men who dress her in long white robes. That's why she's in northern Alberta standing by my desk inspiring me. "Linen —" she snorts. "Retsina ... I'm tired of scrubbing out stains."
    I write deeply moving prose and my muse inspects my room and complains. She sweeps her hand over my shelves. "Is this all you have?" she demands.
    "What kind of literature do you like?" I ask.
    "Literature," she says. "Pooh."
    I give my muse Glamour, Mademoiselle, and the Sears catalogue. She settles down on my bed, peruses shiny fabric, glittery thread.
    I write about humanity and now and then my muse says words aloud — just to hear their sounds. "Revlon Love That Red lipstick," she whispers. "Maybelline Illegal Lengths mascara."
    I write with compassion while she flips the pages. When my work's complete, I read it to her. She shakes her head. "You have to put yourself into it," she says. "Like this —" She stands and declaims

The Winter Catalogue

Let me call up the man at Sears
and order me something — a corset
or black brassieres.

Let it be not-on-sale — money well spent!
that he may know the purity
of my intent.

That though I have — so far — lived by my fears
I now do repent
my careful years.

So let it be lace: easily rent
because yes!
Life should be spent.

She looks at me knowingly. "Write it down," she says. "It's good — it comes from the heart."
I shake my head. "Christ," I say.
"It's uneven — it needs a little work," she agrees. "But it's a start."
"It's not that," I say. "It's just not ... not what I had in mind."
"Not what you had in mind?" my muse says.
She lies back down on the bed and opens another magazine.
"The mind," she says, "is not a good place to begin."

RAVEN MEDITATIONS

1

The thing about the raven is, that it feels no guilt. It has no ego problems, unlike the eagle (the eagle! I could go on for hours about the eagle, who is so fixated on aesthetics, so single-minded and sure of itself and yet what is it but a stinky-breathed fish eater with only the most austere sense of compassion).

But the raven — is so humanly complicated, so intelligent, and takes such pleasure in bothering. It can only squawk and croak — but even its croak has underneath it the sound of water. It is so ugly, an eater of carrion and garbage. There is no romance to the raven.

Maybe it's just that when you reach a certain age, you get tired of romance, aesthetics, elixirs of the mind. The raven has a directness, an ugly, tricky surety. There is no bombast from the raven. You reach a certain age and you can accept the raven's right to jeer at you. You get kind of fond of these catcalls.

The raven is loud and somewhere else
Just the sound of one croak
in the dark cave of his throat
comes out into this
world

For some birds it's a struggle:
they beat their wings quickly — one, two, three times
and then they glide down until they beat again.
Working and resting, they see-saw across the sky.

But for the raven — the sky is all angles
and manipulation. The raven glides up and down
phrasing the rivulets of air or strokes
steadily as if there is someplace to go.

The owl has padded wings,
the poor little mousies have to always
look, look for shadow or movement.
They don't hear anything until it's too late.

But the raven eats dead meat and therefore
he can sit in a tree and call attention to himself.
He's too big to hide or to care
what anyone thinks of him.

So what
if the raven
doesn't
mate for life?
What difference
does it make, knowing that?

When I hear that primitive croak
above these trees, I feel lost.
On this path my husband cut for me,
on the bridges he built for me, I walk
and the forest grows in.

A squad of ravens
patrolling the smoky haze. Reconnoitering a
pink sun, and the light so golden
so roseate. How muffled the trees are
and the grasses.
Somewhere a forest burns
making this gauze.

The ravens — exactly four ravens, glide
through — the tips of their wings
curl up. Each raven's wings beat a measure
as the heart beats its transit.

The falcon — focused
— whether withdrawing in high meditative circles,
his shadow cycling, large and blurry,
or penetrating, focusing in — the shadow
shrinking, becoming more
distinct. Two things, past and future,
rush down into this moment.

The raven flaps
along like an old lady in loose slippers.
She has seen it all — she just wants a cup of coffee.

I could put it in different ways:

1) The raven has a heart and a soul and an ethical structure
   that doesn't mind a little thievery.

2) The raven steals only when he feels
   like it. He isn't compulsive like his cousin,
   Mr. Magpie. Nor does he habitually
   kill baby birds.

3) Caw, caw, caw, the crows say.
   They are also the raven's cousins.
   When you're related to politicians
   and psychopaths, you don't feel bound
   by someone else's moral code.

After the end of the world there will be cockroaches
and ravens. It helps to be omnivorous,
and broad-minded about food. Also to not
be dependent on happiness, to be willing
to scavenge for whatever is there.

Ravens are the remnants of a great civilization.
They have an understanding littered with fallen
columns, potsherds, naves, and
aqueducts that begin and end in sand.
For this reason they aren't easily
impressed. For them, technology is just another
foofaraw, like art and literature.

"You have the cold-hearted intellectual eagle,
the falcon, remote, dispassionate
until confronted with the insight of a mouse;
you have the compulsive woodpecker, the good-hearted chickadee;
you have a whole ecology of personalities
and for what?" the owl asks.

"The raven is blessed. He can both enjoy the world
and live in it."

The raven walks like a swarthy sailor,
swinging from side to side, his feet spread wide:
on leave, with money and time and pride.

Dominus vobiscum
says the raven in the evergreen.
In his domino, with his proboscis with the bits of hairy feathers at its base,
the raven is ridiculous.

Dominus vobiscum
I say back to the raven. It is ridiculous to speak
Latin but the raven likes
dead things and I like the raven.

2

Bury me on a platform in the trees.
Let the birds unravel
what they can. I will
not need it.

Let that part which needed to be whole
find wholeness
in the raven's beak, the sun's light.

Let me disintegrate and join the world from whom
I have held myself apart.

A temporary structure will do:
hitch an undercarriage to the poplars
at a good height. Make it
of tamarack from the burned forest,
the black poles left standing,
kiln-dried and strong, released
from the obligations
of living. Souls on the move,
they will not mind being moved.

Build at a good height,
on trees too slim for a bear to climb;
I don't want to be knocked down
in a heap. For the platform, ask
these trees to lend their branches.
I want to be up there in the flex of things.

Another request before I let you go:
you can use ladders, but no nails,
I don't want to hurt anything anymore.

It will be hard I am sure when the squirrels
scatter my bones, and you see the glint
of my tooth in the magpie's beak—
but this is what I want:
to give back.

This part of me is no longer of use to you—
don't box it up, don't hoard it in the ground
where it can bring happiness to no one.

Let my hair soften a nest or insulate a burrow.
Let the enamel of my tooth satisfy
a foolish obsession — I do not want now
to hinder the world.

Make this platform for me. Build me
the distance I need to become close.

bury me
on a platform in the trees
bury me
in moving air
in light
let the leaves fall on me
and darkness—
let the long winter blanket me
enprism me with snow

You! Raven!
Being of the cloth!
Keeper of the forest!
Attendant at the immaculate altar! Listen to me!

Where is God now?

When all those caravans of ducks and geese, those
pilgrims, have taken their conceptions south —
when the whole show pulls out — what
is left?

Cold flecks the air, we breathe
chips and slivers, and I'm here lurching from tree to tree.

I lean down, I cover my mouth, I build an antechamber
for each breath —

But you call
and I look up
and whose neck
am I stretching?

My very own
idea of God, my first-born
on the altar — a sacrifice
for what? So that I
can see you clearly?

I see you, Raven, head up and sprightly!

Now tell me — what is this
you've obtained?
Presence that doesn't require
or ensure
anything. Presence
without faith, or belief,
or any kind of sanctity
familiar to me.

Where's the salvation?
Where's the escape?
Where's the tattered old
ticket to heaven?

if I were a raven I would ruffle
the ruff at my neck
if I were a chickadee I would
uncache my fat and my protein

I strap on my snowshoes
and make paths
I break trail
again and again
the same trail
a circle, a series of circles,
looping from one to another
and they all end
at our house

trails that begin here, end here

mouse trails that start and end
in a hole

Winter ...
Winter as absence is a delusion I wish I could suppress.

Why do I look elsewhere? What fundamental fault do I have, what blindness of being? What is it in me that makes me so Judas?

With every kiss I bestow identity.

Why do I use you and reject you, how can I have believed that this betrayal was love?

Bury me, yes you should bury me — in a hole, shrouded with all my instructions, all the directions I have provided for how to dispose of a poet, all the ways I elaborate to make myself separate from you.

Help me to be naked truly naked help me to be naked in your love defenseless help me to take until I am submerged in you help me to be merged in you help me to be you you you

Snow, and more snow. Day by day the path
rises. Higher and higher. Beyond brush.
Beyond
what? My head pokes
into an airy place, a distance I do not know.
Under the filigree of branches, a middle place.
On the structure of snow, the surface tense
with cold, I glide up and peer into this opening.

4

Why did
the raven lift me?

I hung there, my bones not hollow, my mind
not hollow.

One shudder at the weight of me and I understood and I
let go.

I would like to say, "the bright light as I fell ..."
but I wasn't high enough for that
or even to be impaled by the trees
and have this thinking pierced.

I wasn't high at all;
I just thumped
down to the ground
as if I had raised my arms
and jumped, thinking I would fly.

The raven swung above me three times, like a censer,
then headed off.

Love is the size of a raven,
thumps out of the air
on to a branch
and grasps firmly.

The branch descends, ascends.
Love flies off and yet the tree
still absorbs
what is no longer there.

Feathers, beak,
skin, eyes, feet
— black drop by black drop —
the branch spreads the raven
down to rootlets, exchanges
love for water.

Love is the shape of a raven,
has wings that end in serrated edges
and a strong torso
and a head dominated by a beak
extruded from the heart like a talon.

love is the colour of a raven
strokes across the white sky
black moment to black moment comes iridescent:
a metallic rasp of blue or green

love twists one shoulder, peers
down from the midst of infinite
distance

from substance: depth
and darkness

with what big wings the raven
embraces the world